oddities oddities oddities
oddities oddities oddities
oddities oddities oddities
oddities oddities oddities
oddities oddities oddities
oddities oddities oddities
oddities oddities oddities
oddities **oddities** oddities
oddities oddities oddities
oddities oddities oddities
oddities oddities oddities
oddities oddities oddities
oddities oddities oddities
oddities oddities oddities
oddities oddities oddities
oddities oddities oddities

a spot the odd one out puzzle book

JOHN BIGWOOD

HARPER
DESIGN
An Imprint of HarperCollins Publishers

Oddities
A Spot the Odd One Out Puzzle Book

Illustrated by John Bigwood
Written by Jonny Leighton
Designed by Derrian Bradder

First published in Great Britain in 2019 by Michael O'Mara Books Limited.
Oddities © 2019 Michael O'Mara Books Limited.

Oddities
Copyright © 2019 Michael O'Mara Books Limited.

HarperCollins books may be purchased for educational, business, or sales promotional use.
For information please email the Special Markets Department at SPsales@harpercollins.com.

First published in 2019 by
Harper Design
An Imprint of HarperCollins Publishers
195 Broadway
New York, NY 10007
Tel: (212) 207-7000
Fax: (855) 746-6023
harperdesign@harpercollins.com
www.hc.com

Distributed throughout North America by
HarperCollins Publishers
195 Broadway
New York, NY 10007

ISBN 978-0-06-295562-3

Printed and bound in the United States of America by LSC Communications.

First U.S. Printing, 2019

19 20 21 PC/LSCC 10 9 8 7 6 5 4 3 2

HOW TO USE THIS BOOK

Simply pick a puzzle and follow the instructions on the
left-hand page. Whether you're finding odd ones out or
matching pairs of oddities, there's plenty to keep your brain
bamboozled on every page, with fun facts along the way.

If you get stuck, all the answers are at the back
of the book. (But who needs those?)

Enjoy!

SPINY SUCCULENTS

Spot the odd one out, if you're sharp enough…

Pulque, made from cactus sap, is a lightly alcoholic,
sour beverage with a yeast-like flavor. Mmm, yeasty booze.
Delicious.

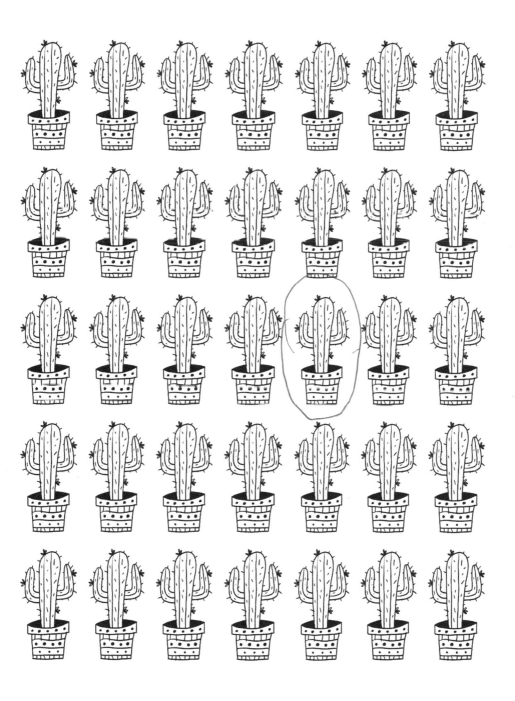

HAPPY HOUR

Separate the three mocktails from the cocktails.

A negroni comprises one part gin,
one part sweet vermouth, and one part Campari.
Oh, and one part hipster…apparently.

DOG DAYS

Find the two cool doggos standing out from the pack.

Greyhounds can reach speeds of 45 miles per hour
and have fantastic vision. Good luck sneaking up on one
of those beady-eyed speed racers.

AWESOME AVO

Spot the pair of odd-vocados among these pitted beauties.

Avocados were originally known as "ahuacate,"
a word derived from the Aztec for testicle.
Still fancy some avocado toast?

FLOWERY FUZZ

Spot the three oddities among these botanical beards.

"Pogonophobia" is the term for an irrational fear
of beards. Or, perhaps it's a rational fear. Who knows
what's lurking inside those hairy face huggers?

HEAVY WEATHER

How many odd waterproof jackets are there
in this collection of coats?

The first waterproof coat was developed by Scottish
chemist Charles Macintosh and was known simply
as a "mac." Don't mistake it for a "mac" computer,
though, they're definitely not waterproof.

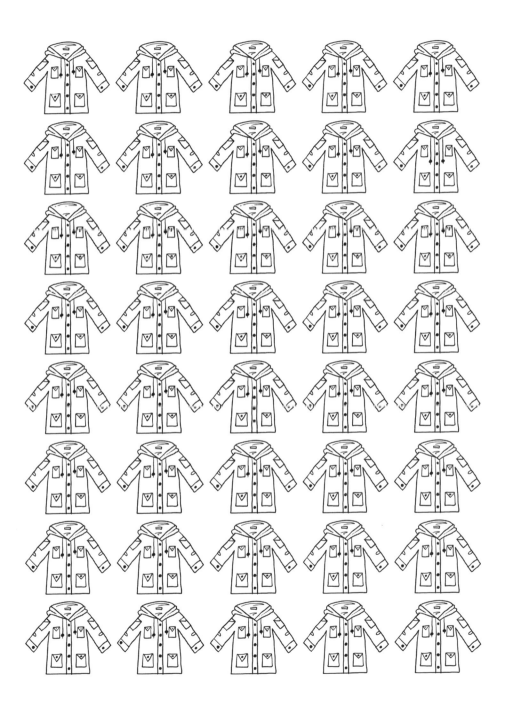

OH DEER

Find the odd stuffed stag hanging on the wall.

The process of taxidermy gained in popularity during
a period in the 18th century known as the Enlightenment,
but it goes back as far as ancient Egypt.
So, no, you didn't like it before anyone else.

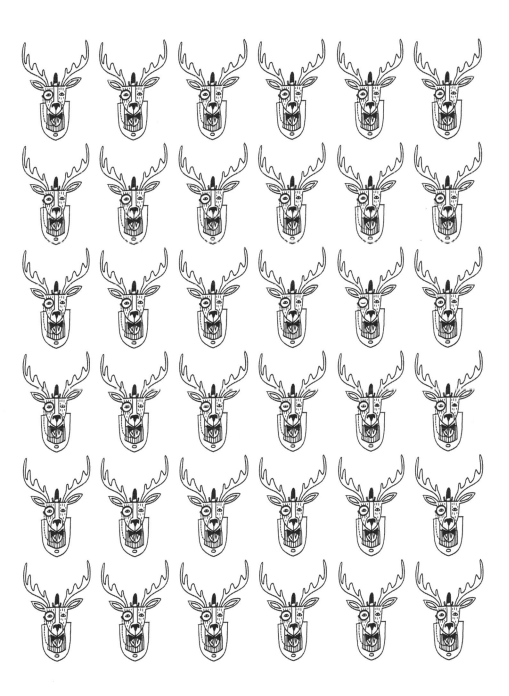

BROKEN RECORD

Don't get into a spin—simply spot the two odd pairs.

The phonograph was created by prolific inventor
Thomas Edison. He also invented the electric lightbulb
and important components for batteries, telegraphs,
the telephone, and motion-picture cameras. What a guy!

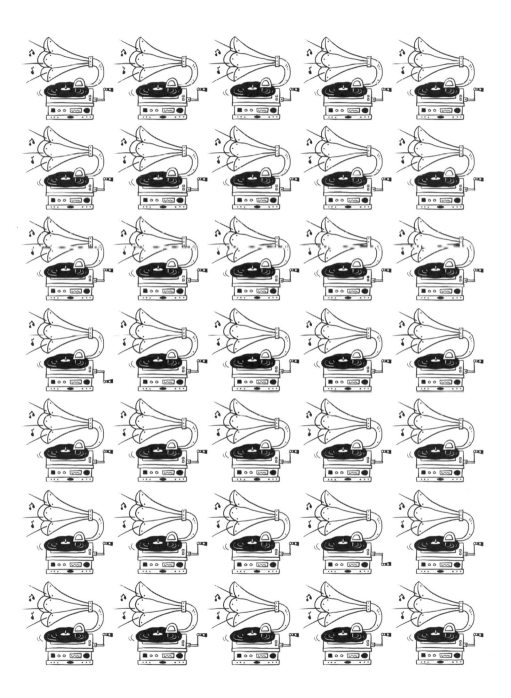

TWERKER BEES

Finger on the buzzer and spot three odd ones out.

Bees can communicate through the power of dance.
They wag their backsides to indicate direction
and distance to food. They basically invented twerking.

AAAND, LIFT!

How many muscle-bound oddities are lurking
among these dumbbells?

Famous Victorian strongman Eugen Sandow was a
bodybuilder and showman from Prussia, who amassed
a vast fortune flexing his muscles and breaking metal
chains with his bare hands. Talk about being ripped!

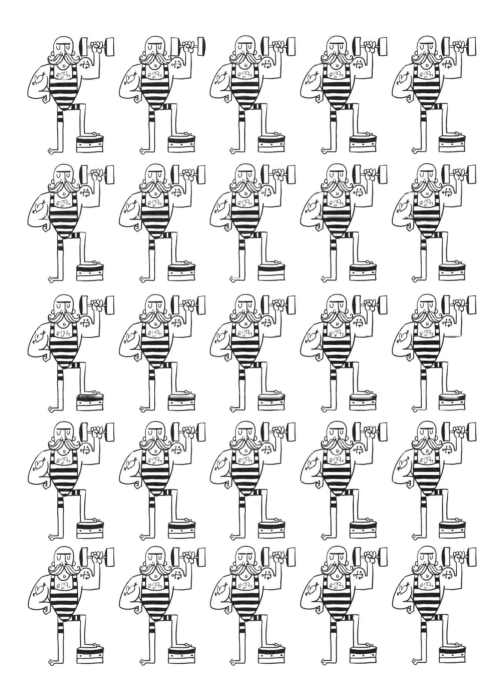

BORN TO BE MILD

Spot the five particular pandas in this lineup.

Bamboo makes up more than 90 percent of a panda bear's
diet and they spend up to 16 hours a day
eating the stuff. No wonder they're going extinct;
they don't have time to do anything else.

PEDAL POWER

Fix up and look sharply for the three odd bikes out.

Bicycles have gone by a lot of odd names over the
years, particularly in the early days when they
were alternatively known as velocipedes, hobby horses,
pedestrian curricles, and even "boneshakers."

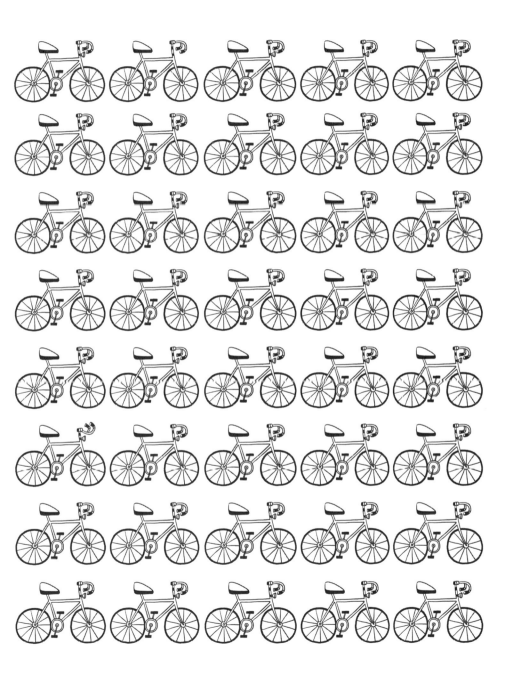

PANGOLIN PARTY

Find the two odd pangolin pairs.

The name pangolin comes from the Malay word for
"rolling over," referring to the animal's habit of
rolling into a ball when threatened. Their other means
of defense is to emit odor from their anal glands.
So, "pangolin" really was the better choice of name.

MMM, TACOS...

Find the three odd pairs among these tortilla treats.

Tacos comprise of tortillas folded around a
spicy filling of meat, fish, beans, or cheese, perfect
to munch on during a mid-puzzle snack attack.

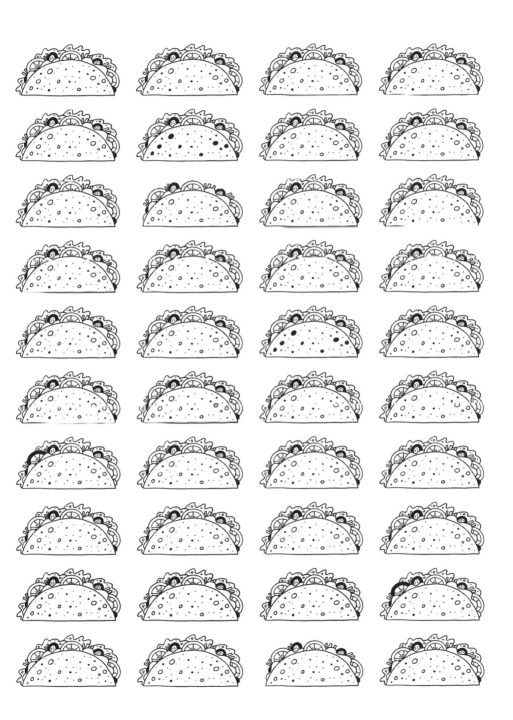

CAMP IT UP

Each happy camper van has a pair—match all twelve.

The record for the longest driven journey goes to Emil and
Liliana Schmid who have been on a camper-vanning
odyssey since 1984, traveling across 186 countries. It's possible
they're taking the concept of a gap year a bit too far.

IN A FLAP

Find four odd ones out among these plucky pigeons.

Homing pigeons—unlike their urban cousins, the rock
doves—are able to sense Earth's magnetic field and
use it for navigation. They basically have superpowers.

JUST MY TYPE

Look closely and find the two odd ones out.

Mark Twain was the first author to submit a
manuscript composed on a typewriter. He also loved cats.
These two facts aren't related.

GET THE HORN

Spot the unique unicorn among these magical creatures.

The collective noun for a group of unicorns is a "blessing"
(a "fact" so sweet you might just vomit a rainbow).

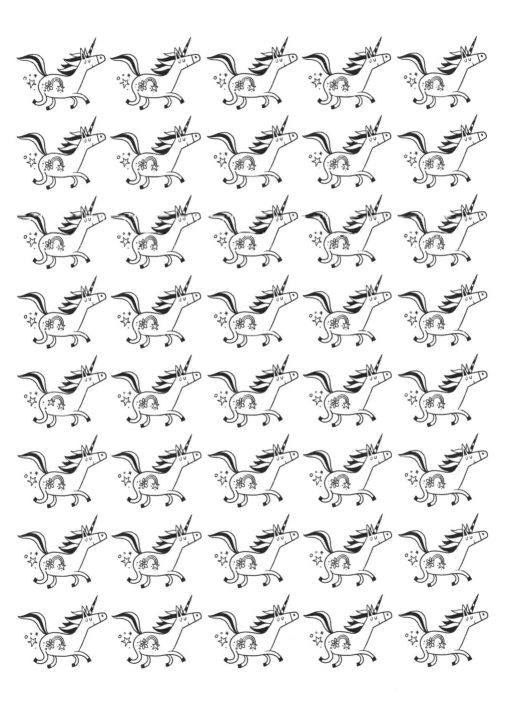

LLAMA DRAMA

Spot the odd pair among these llamas with lluscious llocks.

When frustrated, llamas are notorious for
spitting, hissing, and kicking. Much like puzzlers
who can't find the odd ones out.

CAP FLAP

How many odd ones out are there among these cool caps?

Back in the day, some cyclists put cabbage leaves
under their "casquettes" to keep their heads cool.
Time to bring back the trend, right?

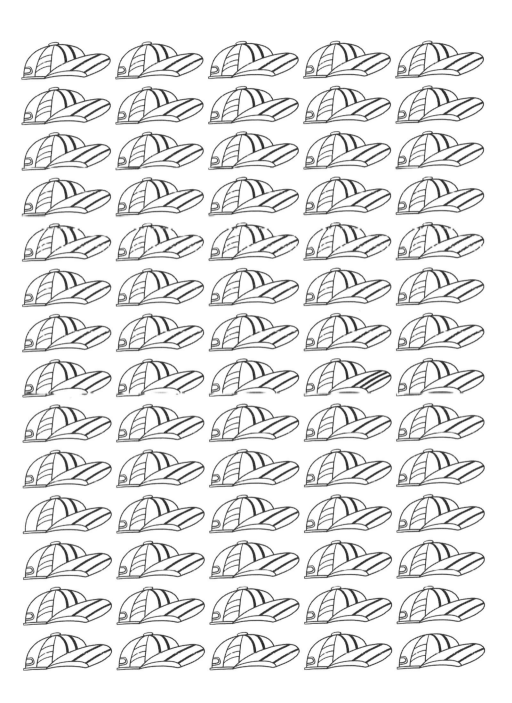

SUGAR OVERLOAD

Spot the four odd desserts among these sweet treats.

Freak shakes, with their combination of milkshake,
ice cream, doughnuts, cake, and toppings, are so sweet that
they might just give unicorns a run for sickliness.

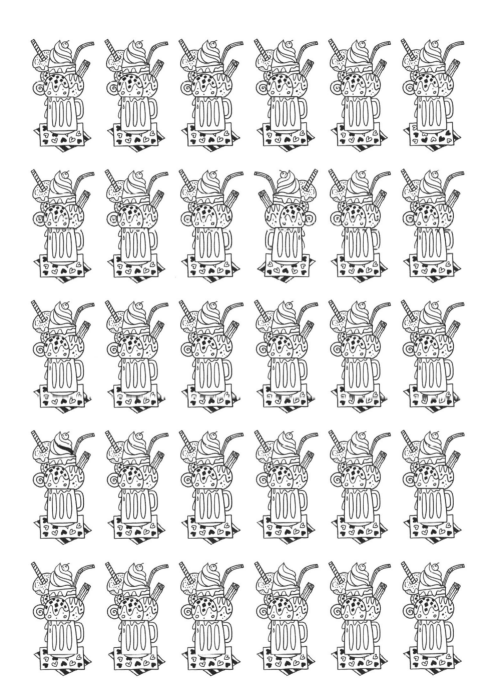

THINK INK

Spot the odd tat-twos out.

The famous "Leopard Man of Skye," Tom Leppard,
was so-named due to the leopard print tattoos
that covered 99.9 percent of his body. There'd be no
trouble spotting him in the wild.

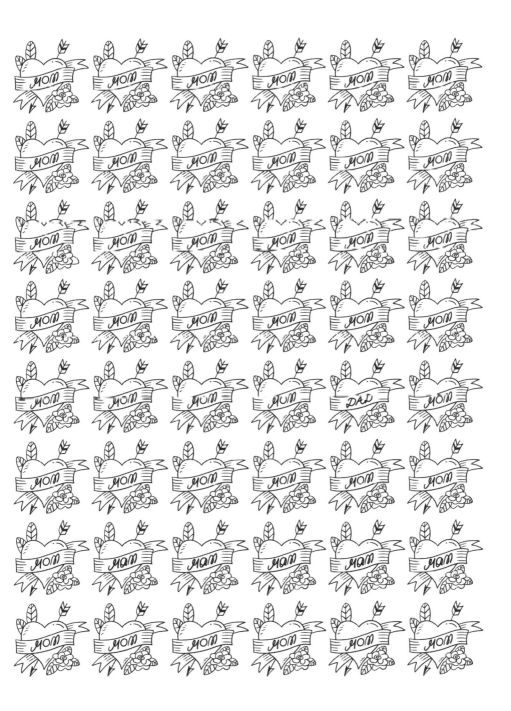

CAT'S MAGIC

Find the four odd toms lurking among
these keyboard kitties.

Tabby cats descend from a sacred
breed worshipped by the ancient Egyptians.
No wonder they're so superior.

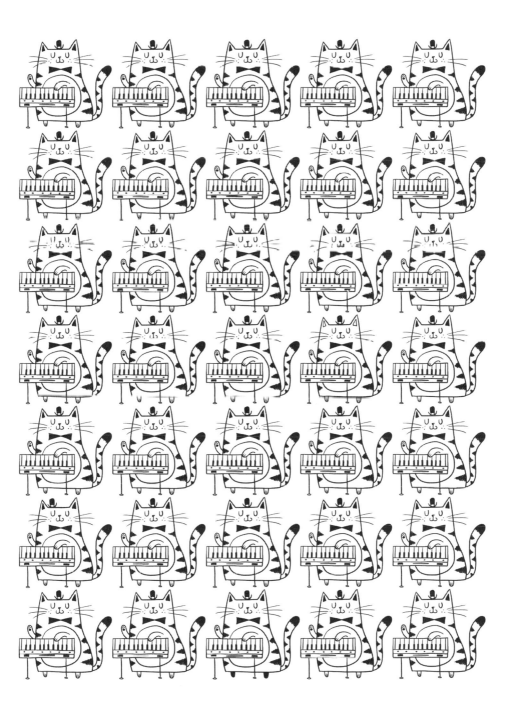

KEEN BEAN

Find the odd-uccino among these caffeinated cups.

Legend has it that coffee was discovered when an Arab
goatherd noticed how hyperactive his flock became
after eating the berries of an evergreen bush. Naturally he
tried them himself and coffee was born!

BONE HEAD

Spot the two pairs of odd skulls.

Sugar skulls are used as decoration on the
Day of the Dead, a traditional Mexican holiday
that honors the dead and confronts death
head-on. Or perhaps skull-on, in this instance.

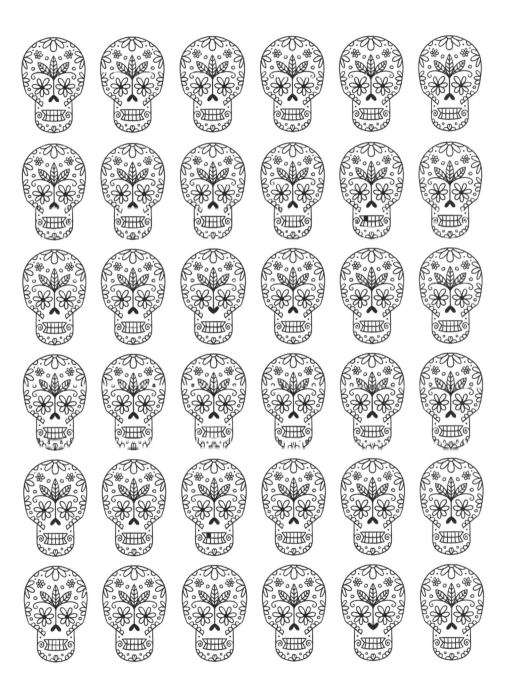

STOMP STOMP

Don't get tied up in knots; spot the odd one out.

Hard-wearing, punky work boots are the perfect
way to express your individuality. So much so that
literally everyone has a pair.

SPECS APPEAL

Focus hard and find the odd one out.

Legend has it that Roman emperor Nero once used emerald
instead of glass in an early type of sunglasses; the stone's
green hue apparently helped cut down glare from the sun.
And people said he was extravagant...Pfft!

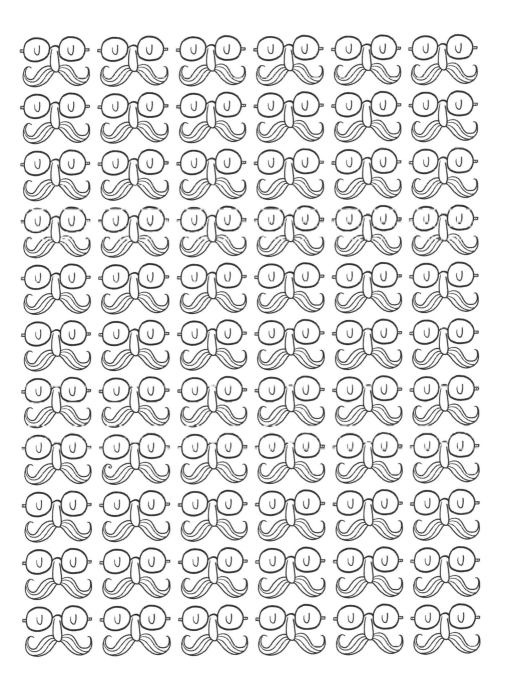

IT'S A HOOT

Spot the four odd owls among these feathery gliders.

Screech owls perform duets across the trees,
with the males and females each
having distinctive songs. How romantic!

PLAY THE FOOL

Spot the three odd pairs. No joke.

The fool, or the jester, was a type of comedic entertainer
whose zany style meant he could make fun of everyone
from kings to paupers. So, watch out, millennials.

SNAP HAPPY

Point and click at the three odd ones out.

The word "photography" is derived from two Greek
words and means "to draw with light." So, in a way,
every selfie is a light drawing. Kinda.

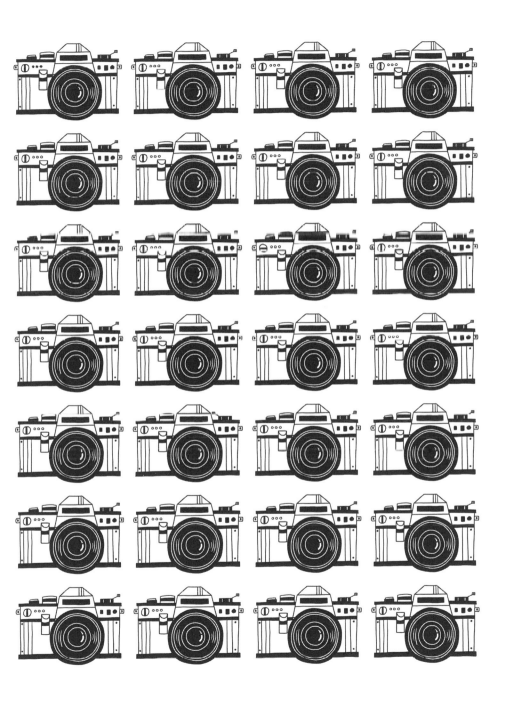

NICE SLICE

Spot the two odd toppings on these pizza pies.

The longest pizza in the world measured more than
a whopping 6,332 feet and took 100 people 54 hours to
create. Goodness knows how they delivered it...

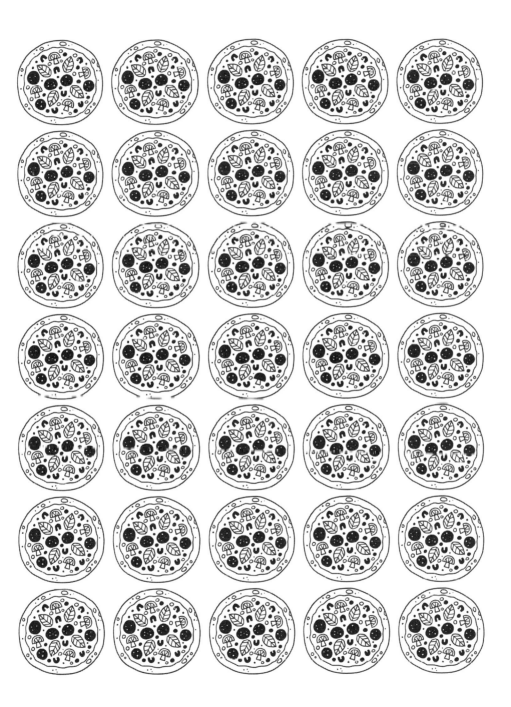

SLO-MO SLOTH

Take your time and spot the two odd pairs
of chilled-out sloths.

Sloths are closely related to the other sinful animals:
envy, pride, greed, gluttony, lust, and wrath. You don't want
to meet a wrath in the wild, that's for sure.

BOOT UP

Give it some wellies and find the three odd ones out.

The average distance walked by a Glastonbury festivalgoer is 9.38 miles. Not bad going in all that mud.

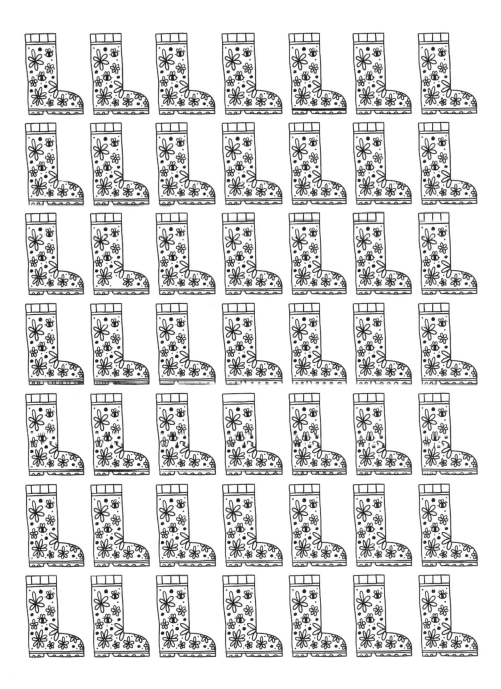

PENNY PINCHING

Spot the three odd pairs among these very vintage bikes.

Penny-farthing bicycles were so named in reference
to the largest and smallest coins of late-Victorian Britain.
A lesser-known nickname was "death trap."

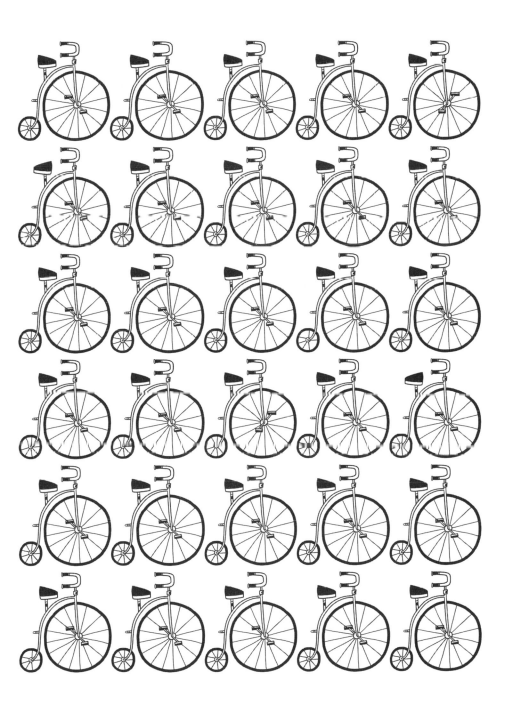

CLOSE SHAVE

Make a dash for the two odd 'staches.

In ancient Rome, moustaches without beards were
seen as the height of barbarism. And yet, fighting lions
to the death was cool. Strange times.

TIME'S UP

Take your time finding the odd one out.

Sadly, it's not possible to go back in time. The hours spent doing this puzzle book are gone for good, never to return. It's a sobering thought, sobering indeed.

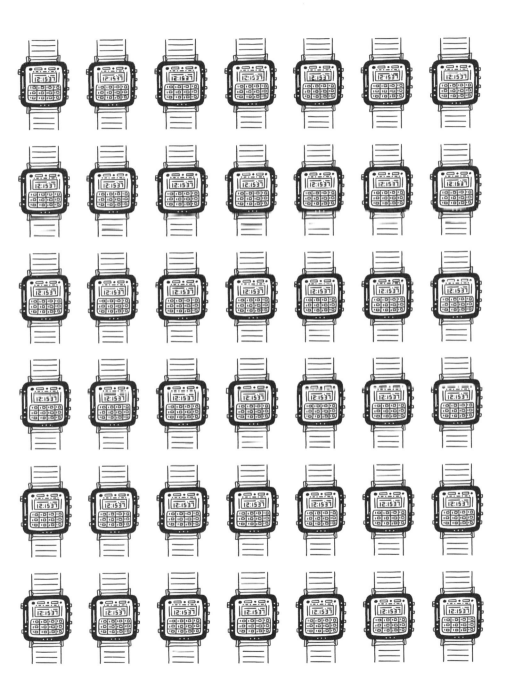

BRIGHT SPARK

Flip the switch on the three odd ones out.

The longest-lasting light bulb has been burning
in a fire station in California since 1901. That's the
same year that Theodore Roosevelt became
US president and Queen Victoria died!

TWISTED TENTACLES

Spot the two odd pairs in this sea of octopuses.

The common octopus is thought to be the most intelligent of all invertebrate animals. It can also change the color of its skin to camouflage itself from predators, making it even harder to spot the odd ones out.

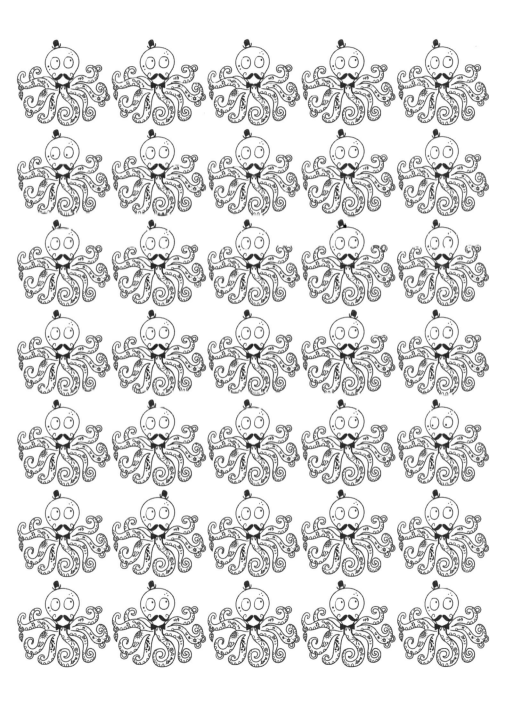

CAB FAB

Hail the three odd cabs among these cranky taxis.

Cab drivers in London must pass a test called
"the Knowledge," memorizing thousands of streets
and landmarks in the center of the city. It makes
guessing the odd one out seem like a piece of cake.

INSTANT SNAP

Spot the two snap-happy odd pairs lurking among these pics.

Artists David Hockney, Keith Haring, and Andy Warhol
have all used Polaroids to prepare or create their work.
Say "cheese!"

COCO LOCO

Relax with a cocktail in a coconut and spot the two odd ones out.

Apart from being a delicious fruit, coconuts also lend
their name to a type of crab, so called for their impressive
ability to crack open the husks with ease. Coconut crabs
are not to be messed with.

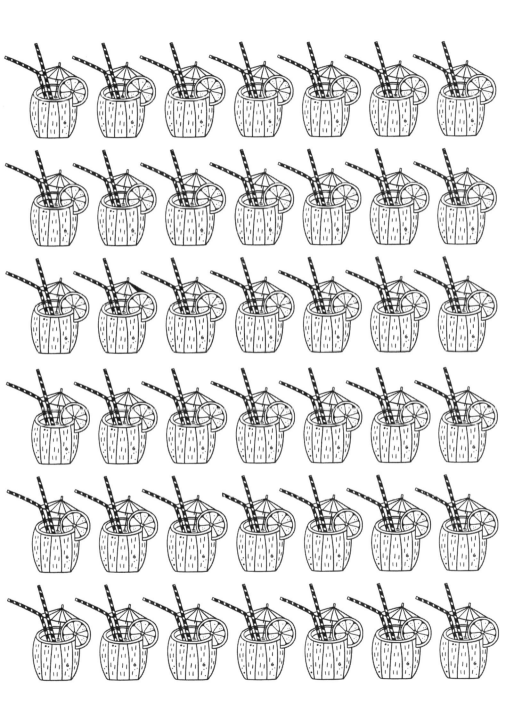

SIMPLE STYLE

Spot the four odd ones out among these trendy tables.

Mid-20th century furniture is known for its
chic simplicity, effortless cool, and timeless design.
Oh, and being achingly on trend, of course.

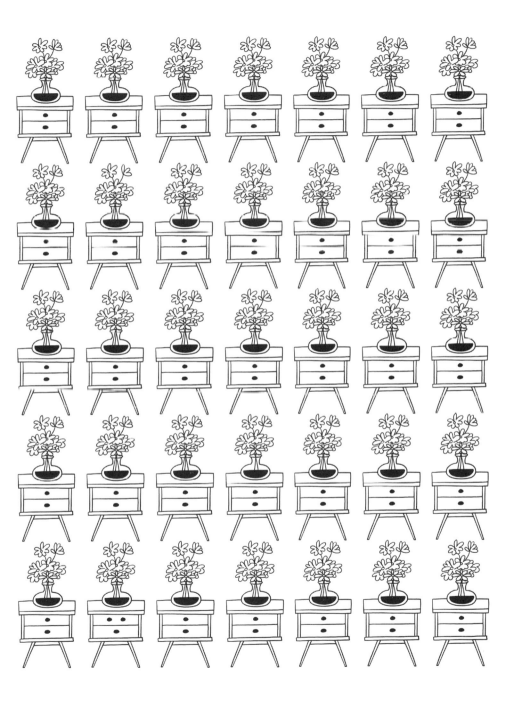

KEEP ROLLIN'

Spot the odd pair of wheels among these speedy rollers.

Some of the earliest roller skates were invented
back in the 1760s by Belgian pioneer Joseph Merlin.
Pity he couldn't conjure up some brakes, which
weren't developed until the 1850s.

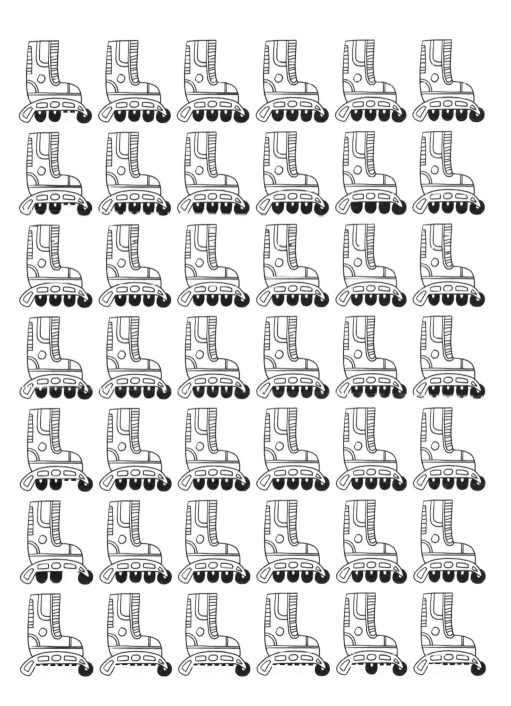

TROPICAL TWIST

Find the three odd pineapple pairs among these juicy fruits.

Pineapple juice can be used in a wide range of cocktails,
most notably the piña colada where it's combined
with delicious coconut cream and white rum. Cheers!

ALL THE ANSWERS

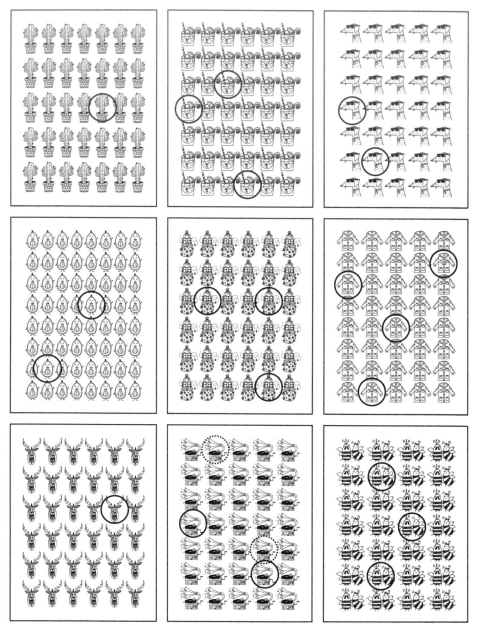

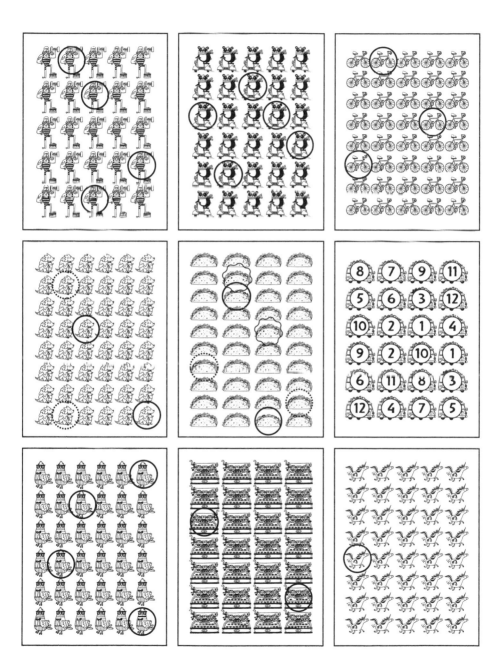

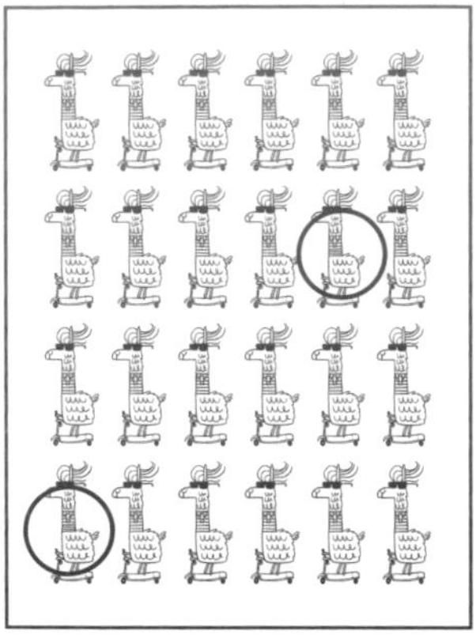
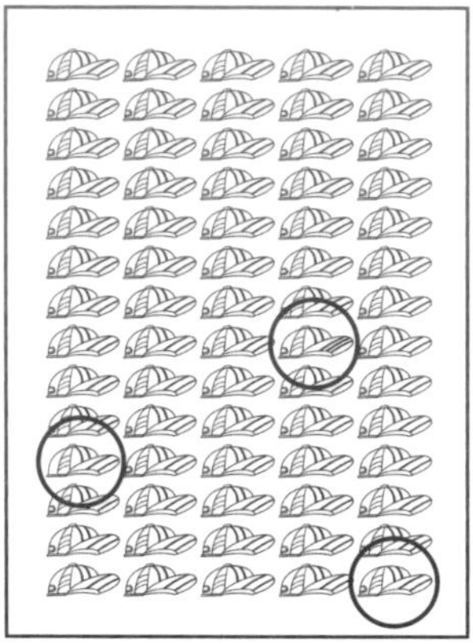
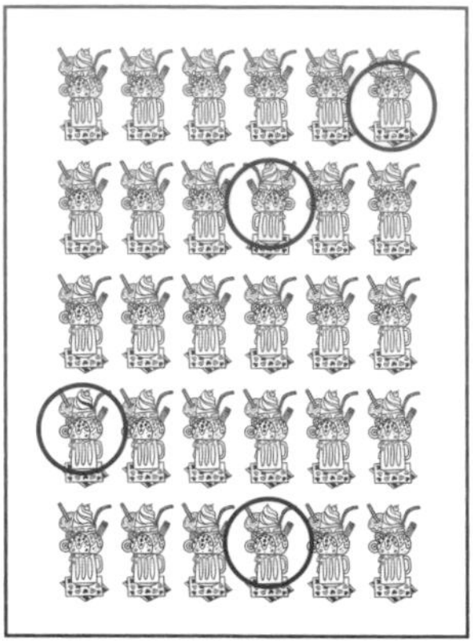
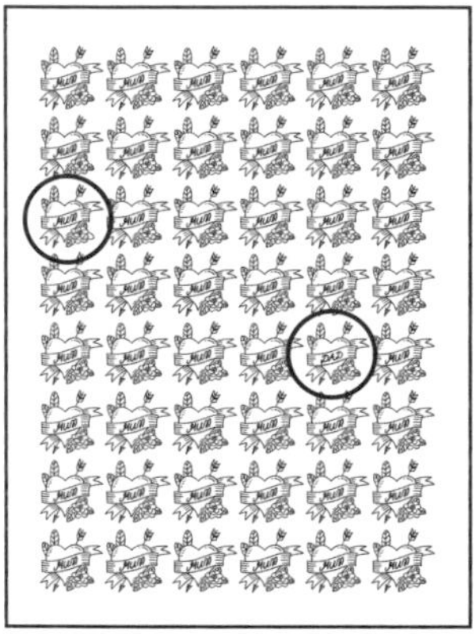
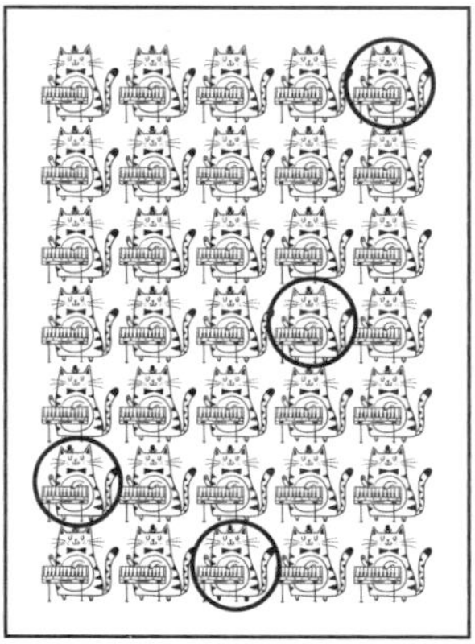
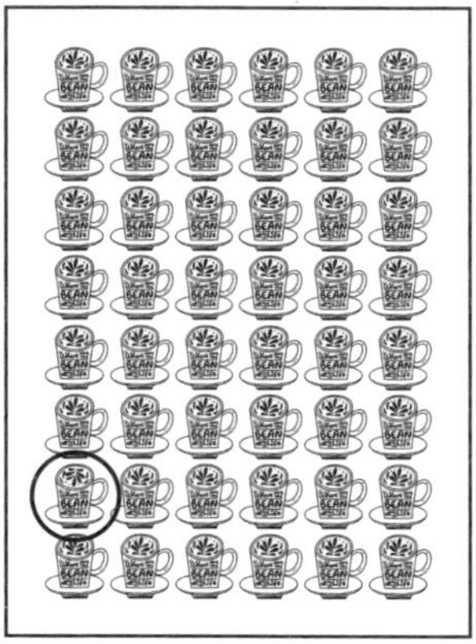
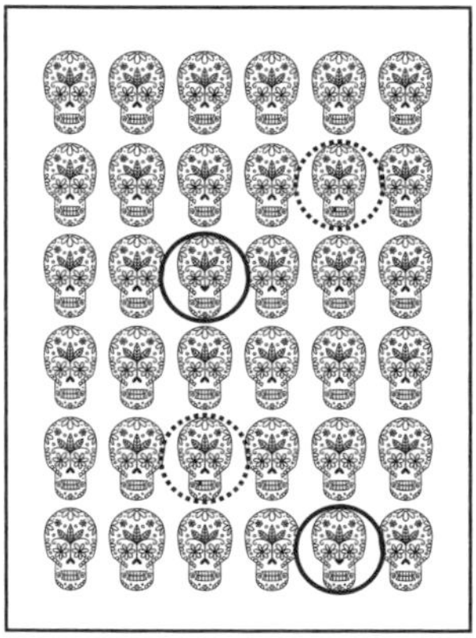
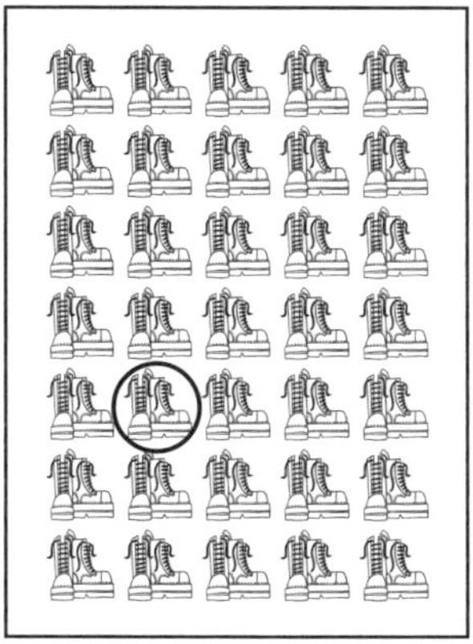
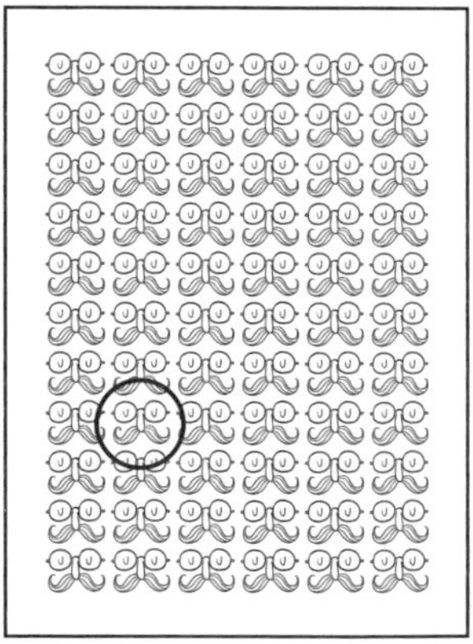

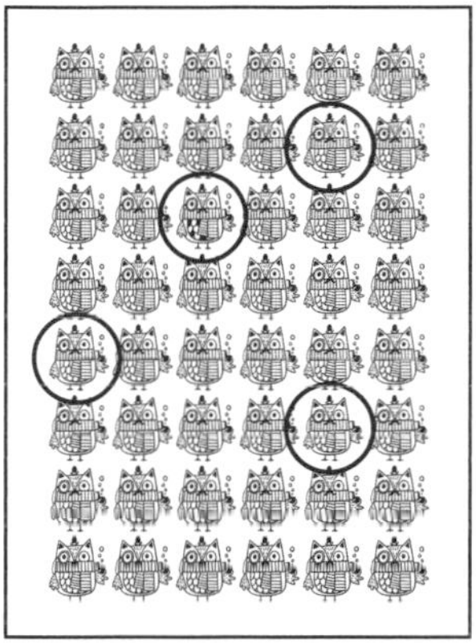
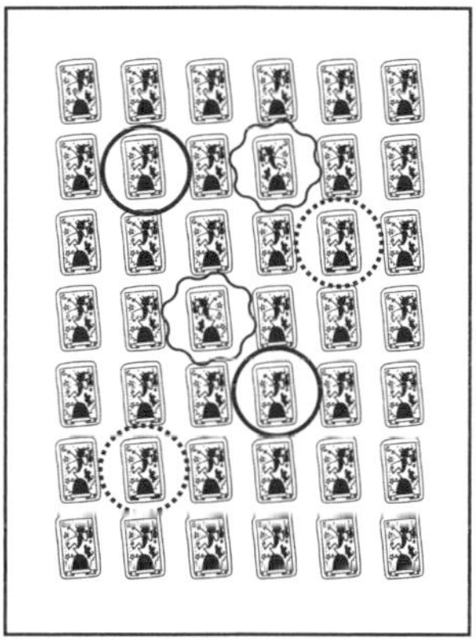
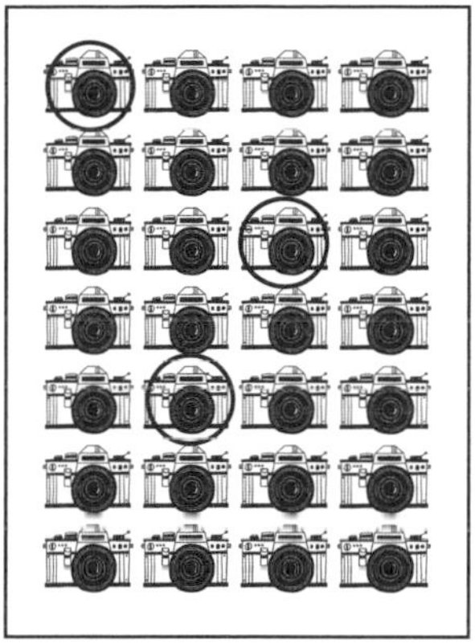
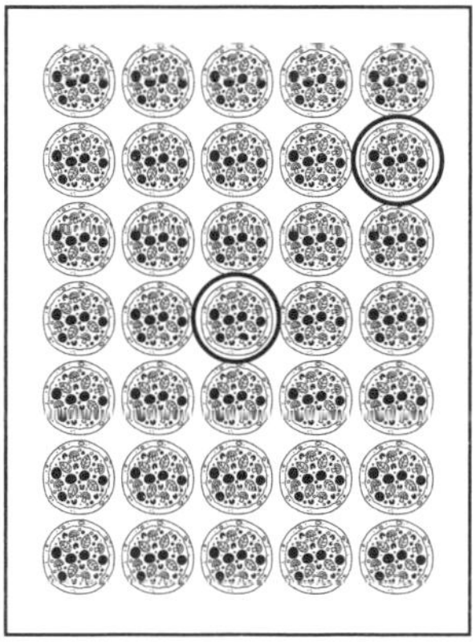
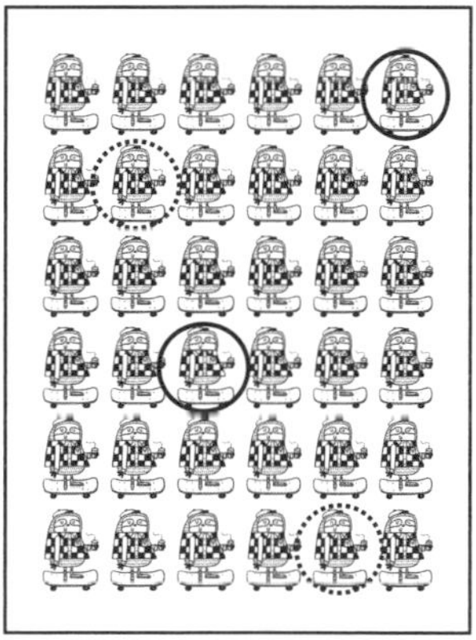
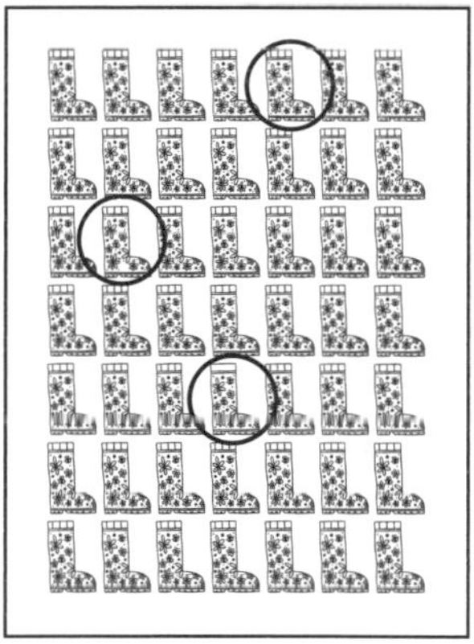
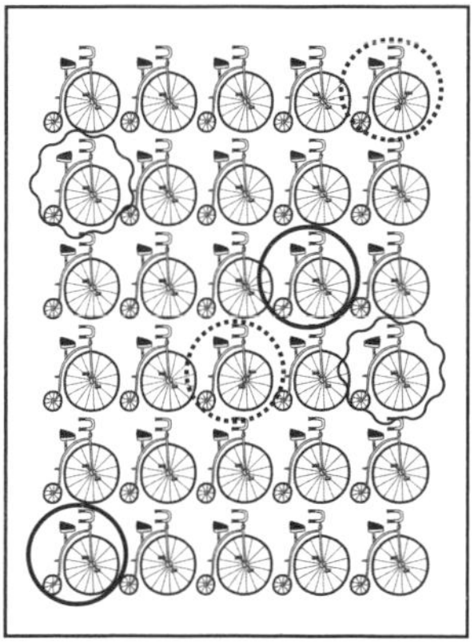
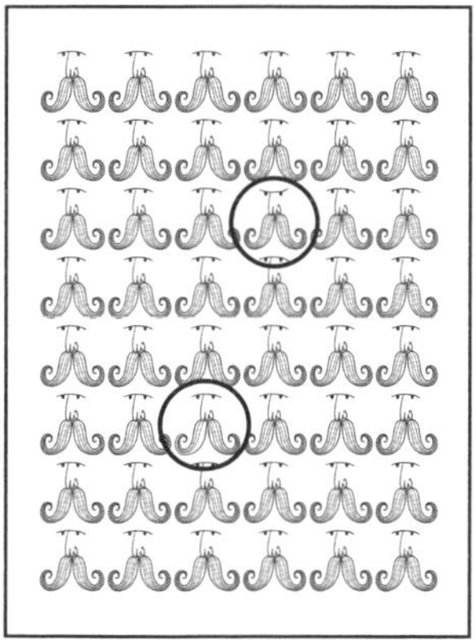
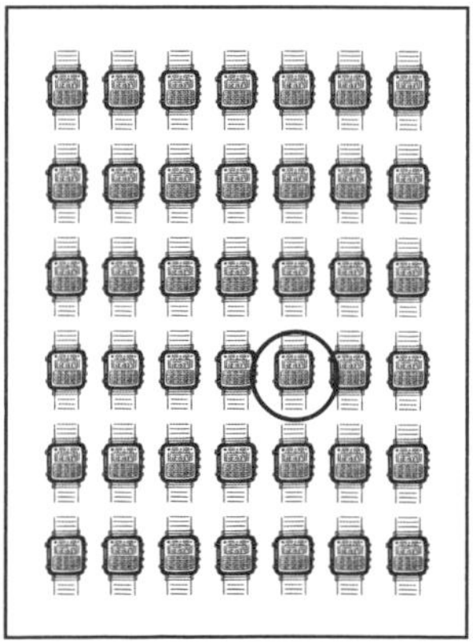

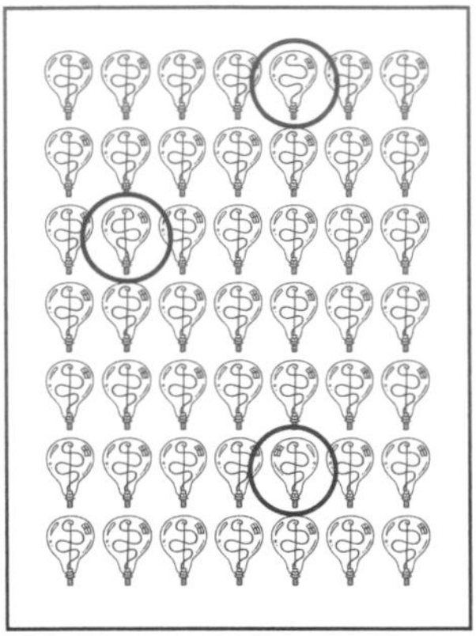

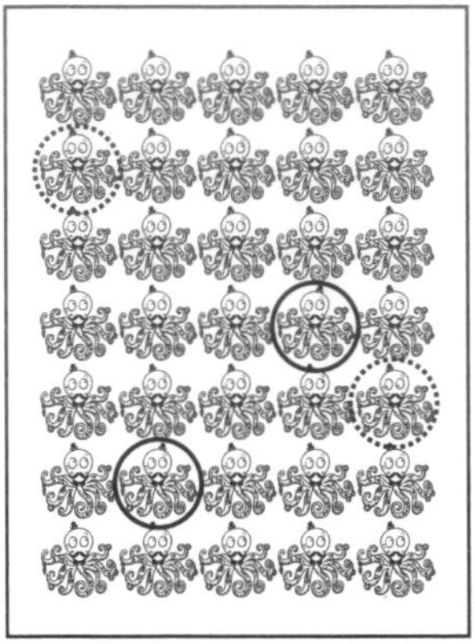

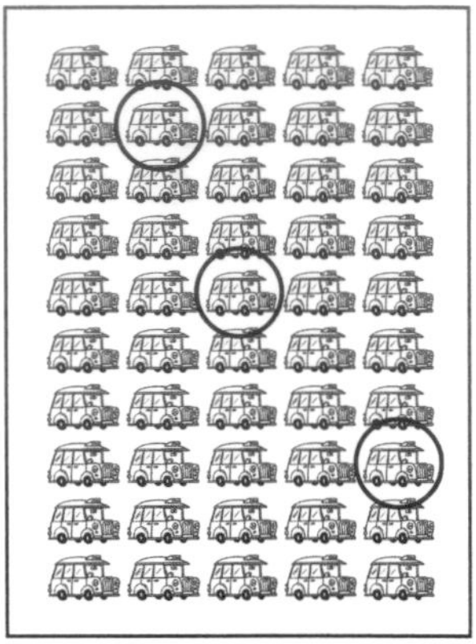

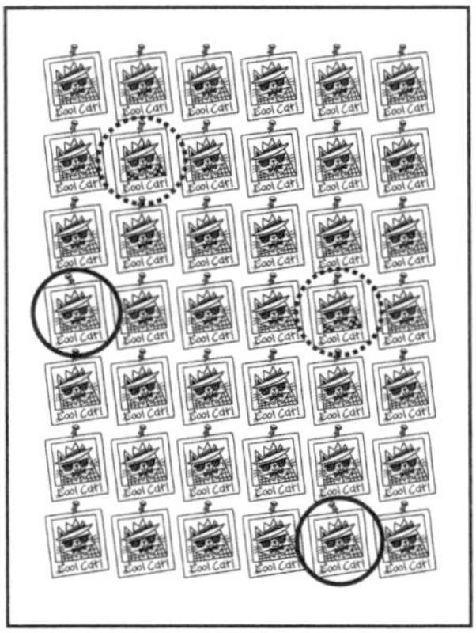
Cool Cat!

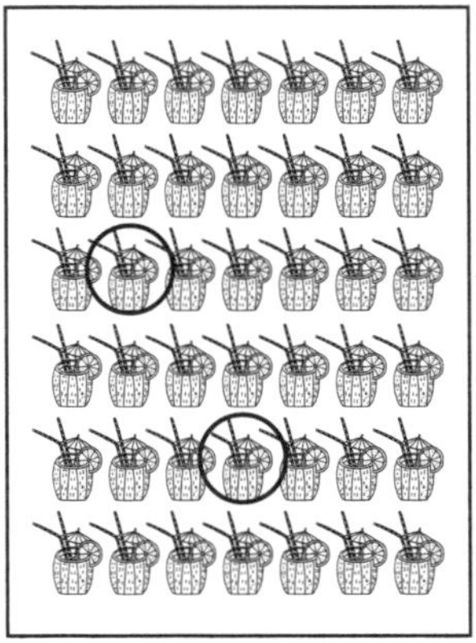

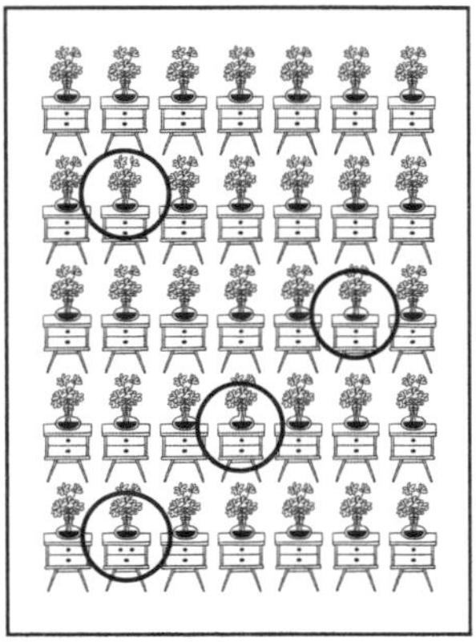

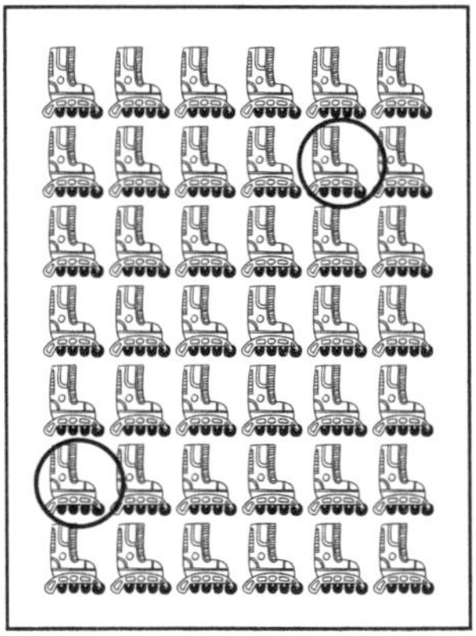

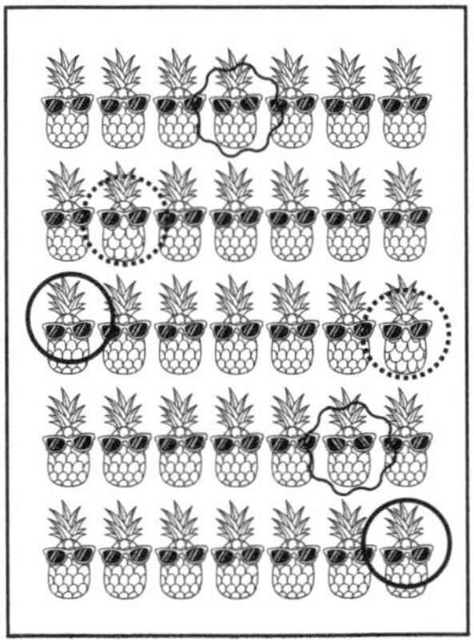

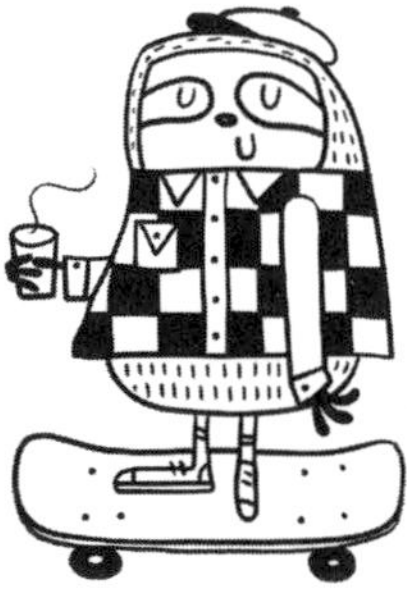